# THE EVOLUTION OF YOUNG CHRISTIANS

**COLLIECIA WRIGHT**

THE EVOLUTION OF YOUNG CHRISTIANS. Copyright © 2021. Colliecia Wright. All Rights Reserved.

No portion of this book may be reproduced, stored in a retrieval system, or transmitted in any form or by any means, except for brief quotations in printed reviews, without the prior written permission of DayeLight Publishers or Colliecia Wright.

Published by

ISBN: 978-1-953759-30-6 (paperback)

Interior Layout and Book Cover Design by DayeLight Publishers.

Scripture taken from the New King James Version®. Copyright © 1982 by Thomas Nelson. Used by permission. All rights reserved.

Scripture quotations marked (NIV) are taken from the Holy Bible, New International Version®, NIV®. Copyright © 1973, 1978, 1984, 2011 by Biblica, Inc.™ Used by permission of Zondervan. All rights reserved worldwide. www.zondervan.com The "NIV" and "New International Version" are trademarks registered in the United States Patent and Trademark Office by Biblica, Inc.™

Scripture quotations marked (NLT) are taken from the Holy Bible, New Living Translation, copyright © 1996, 2004, 2007 by Tyndale House Foundation. Used by permission of Tyndale House Publishers, Inc., Carol Stream, IL 60188. All rights reserved.

Scripture quotations marked "KJV" are taken from the Holy Bible, King James Version (Public Domain).

Scripture quotations marked "ESV" are from the ESV Bible® (The Holy Bible, English Standard Version®), copyright © 2001 by Crossway Bibles, a publishing ministry of Good News Publishers. Used by permission. All rights reserved.

# DEDICATION

I dedicate this book to God my creator, sustainer and guide, without whom, its creation would not be possible. He gave me the wisdom, understanding and strength to toil through hours of laborious thinking and writing, which I'm now sharing with you.

*Father, you are my everything. I continue to pursue you and ask you to help me to allow my life to be reflective of you now and always.*

I also dedicate this book to every young person who wants to write a book or is in the process of doing so. Don't ever doubt that you can. I am a living witness that it is possible. I'm trusting that it will be an inspiration to you. God bless you!

## ACKNOWLEDGEMENTS

I say a heart-felt thanks to my parents and support team for your unwavering support as you stood by my side on every step of the way in this process. You were a tower of strength when I got weary. I could not have asked for a better support team. I love you all endlessly.

A special thanks to my editor Heather Davis, who agreed to review my writing without hesitation and provided invaluable insights to make this more reader-friendly. God bless you.

# TABLE OF CONTENTS

*Dedication* ............................................................................ *iii*

*Acknowledgements* ....................................................... *v*

*Foreword* ............................................................................ *9*

*Introduction* ................................................................... *11*

*Chapter 1: The Pressures Young Christians Face* .......... *13*

*Chapter 2: How to Overcome* ........................................ *27*

*Chapter 3: The Balance* ................................................. *33*

*Chapter 4: Walking Boldly as Young Christians* ............ *37*

*Chapter 5: Making an Impact* ........................................ *43*

*Chapter 6: Maintaining a Fueled Christian Life* ............ *47*

*Concluding Statements* ................................................. *57*

*Notes* ............................................................................... *58*

# FOREWORD

"If you are always trying to be normal, you'll never know how amazing you can be" - Maya Angelou.

I have watched Colliecia's growth from her early childhood years, through to her transition into a young woman who displays extraordinary talents and gifts beyond her years. She has a bold and witty persona that endears her immediately to her peers and older adults alike. I am proud to see that she has blossomed into a wise soul that distinguishes herself with poise, self-awareness and diligence in the things of Christ.

It's no surprise to me then, that Colliecia has written this book. As an author myself, I am aware of the courage required to take so bold a step, especially if the content of your work makes you vulnerable. However, being aware of Colliecia's own tenacity, this compelling work falls in line with my high expectations of one so bold. I am further certain, that the messages shared in this book will resonate with young adults and provide useful tips for their own development.

Colliecia validates the challenges and hardships that youth face as real and important. In this book, The Evolution of Young Christians, she writes to help young people, especially young Christians, discover the power of faith and the value of healthy spiritual development rooted in the teachings of Christ. Colliecia writes of the importance of constantly absorbing challenges and being persistent in repeated efforts even after failure. Her experiences encourage a spiritual resilience that she has proven as her own foundation in her Christian journey.

This book will help you to understand, that despite the pressures that you may face on your Christian journey, you can still find balance and create an impact in the Kingdom of God.

My prayer is that every reader will be left activated to continue their journey, knowing that it is possible. As the word of God says "With man this is impossible, but with God all things are possible." Matthew 19:26.

I fully endorse this work and look forward to great things to come in the future.

*Sophia Gabriel-Barrett*

# INTRODUCTION

Dawnchere Wilkerson posited, *"Don't discount your story, God will use the broken pieces of your life to heal someone else."* As far back as I can remember, I have loved writing and it was always one of my main goals to write a book. I never knew exactly what I would write about. Added to that, I have always been discounting my story, not realizing that all along God had already given me my novel.

I've had many of my peers look up to me as a young Christian. I know firsthand that being a young Christian is not easy, because I've had some weary, tiring days and some 'hard hills to climb' as we say in Jamaica. It is my intent, that sharing stories of my journey with my peers and with others, will extend the conversation about the pitfalls and concerns that many young people face. Importantly this is an encouragement to everyone that it can all be overcome. It's all about our evolution, the persons we are becoming. It will all work out for our good in the end. I am not just saying that. That is a promise of our Heavenly Father.

I have found that for me, and many young Christians, balancing Christian life with other aspects of life can be challenging. This book encourages and challenges young persons and persons new to the faith as they figure out their Christian journey.

This book is also for those persons who feel very timid in their Christian wlk but have a desperate desire to be bold. It will not only state facts, but will provide solutions and encouragement specifically for young Christians and young people in general who are striving to evolve. Be not discouraged. You are not too young to be great. There is light at the end of the tunnel. Read on and be blessed!

# CHAPTER I

# THE PRESSURES YOUNG CHRISTIANS FACE

"Blessed is the one who perseveres under trial because, having stood the test, that person will receive the crown of life that the Lord has promised to those who love him." James 1:12 (NIV)

I remember this difficult time in my life like it was yesterday. It was my final year in high school. I was really happy to be coming to the end of this stage in my education journey. The year went by so quickly and before I realized, it was time for my Caribbean Secondary Education Certificate (CSEC) exams. I was doing 10 subjects and I prepared really hard.

There was this one exam in particular for which I intensely prepared because that subject had been a sticking point during the year. Success at this stage didn't feel optional since so much of my future pursuits were dependent on these grades. This one subject would determine the next step I would take towards my professional goals. I did my exams in May and June and I was very confident that I would get really great pass-marks. Now for the nail-biting finish! I had to wait for the results.

Well, time seemed to have been cooperating with me because before I knew it, August came and like a packaged deal, with it came time for me to see my results. I was so nervous. I thought I would throw up. "I can do this! I can do this!" I thought as I scrolled through my results. I was pleased with what I was seeing until I reached the end of the page and saw it. I failed.

So many thoughts flashed through my mind in an instant, but the reality was that I failed one of the most crucial subjects, the same one I needed for the next step in my academic plan. I was devastated. I wanted to wake up from this horrible nightmare. I became depressed for months and lessened my communication with others. Some people who I thought would be in my life forever left because they felt like I wasn't there when they needed me. They didn't know what was going on and I was not in the frame of mind to explain. I had to take care of myself before attempting to address others.

I was upset with God. So upset that I found it really difficult to pray. Actually, I didn't. Neither did I engage in worship. It was so bad I didn't even want to participate in activities at church. Those who stood by my side through this hard time kept on saying "trust God", but I kept on wondering how can I trust the same person who failed me? They also said "It's just one subject, you can pick it up again." But I thought, "Pick up again when the plans I had for my future have already been stripped away?" Notice I kept saying "I" and not "God". This was the problem.

I made plans for my life but I didn't make plans for His will. He says that He knows the plans He has for my life so how could I be making plans without thinking about whether or not it was His will?

I came to understand, that as Christians, though we may make huge plans for our lives, if it's not the will of God, these plans will not be fruitful. God's plan for our lives is bigger than we can ever imagine but sometimes we allow our plans to be a big blur over His.

## **GOD IS IN CONTROL**

When I started my Christian journey at the age of 10, I assumed that it would be just a simple 1+1 mathematical equation. But this was not the case. As I grew in my journey, the challenges came and I came to realize that this journey was never going to be the fairytale I imagined. I must tell you, it won't be a fairytale for you either.

I was troubled on every side because being a Christian did not change the struggles my family had to go through to ensure that we had what we needed to survive economic hardships. It didn't change the violence that I witnessed in my society at times or the misfortunes of others that I loved. What Christianity gave me however, was a perspective through which to see these things and an assurance that God was in control even if I didn't understand the circumstances around me.

You see, God is still God, even if we disagree with him. When we do not understand our circumstances, He is not less God either! To add, my mother always reminded me that we didn't need to be distressed, because God would see us through. The added assurance of my mother was a blessing that reinforced the harsh truth of my Christian reality. God is in control. Like, for real, Him alone.

The acknowledgement of this control and the submission required did not come without a hefty social price tag. I was teased and mocked by some of my peers at school who questioned why I wanted to be a Christian at so early a stage. Somehow for them, Christianity was this mystery that should only be undertaken well after youthful exuberance had faded into a kind of adult sobriety that was way more fitting.

There would be whispers and catty remarks just out of my earshot and some would dare to even say to my face that I would give up my faith in a year's time. But I could not be shaken. I was constantly reminded of the fact that I was not forsaken and that others were on this journey too, who had endured worst and still persevered in faith. I was not alone. And neither are you.

## PRESSURE?

What are these so-called pressures anyway? Surely, failing an exam or being teased is a part of life. So do young Christians face real pressures? Well, the brief answer is yes. Even if those older in age and stage cannot identify with the issues that trouble us, that doesn't make them less valid. Does a matter cause you distress or challenges your faith? Then that's important! No matter how small or insignificant it is made to seem, that is valid to you and therefore valid to God.

In fact, often, it is the small issues of the early years of life that grow and fester into major challenges that derail us as we get older. We ignore simple habits, or we delay dealing with stress and carry these issues with us into adulthood. So again, yes, young people face pressures!

In addition, young Christians face some of the very same pressures more mature Christians face. We deal with peer pressure, drugs, issues of sexuality, anxiety, self-doubt and a major one, fear. Fear of the unknown, fear of not measuring up, fear of being labelled a failure, fear of not fitting in, fear of being different, fear of disappointment, among others.

These pressures are usually not easy to deal with, because of limited spiritual experience or social constraints. In fact, they can cause a young Christian to question their purpose, their salvation, God's love for them, even question whether they are fully equipped for the Christian journey.

I have laid out 10 of the most common issues that my friends and I faced growing up as Christians. I have put practical, proven solutions with each issue that helped us all to be better. I hope it works for you too!

| The Issue | What to Do | Reference |
|---|---|---|
| Sexual temptation | Just move. Move away from that space of sexual temptation or you will be trapped. You will feel better knowing that you have escaped another trap of the enemy and remained obedient to God. | 2 Timothy 2:22 |
| Peer Pressure | Nothing is wrong with getting some new friends. Sometimes God places some persons in our lives to teach us what not to do. | Proverbs 13:20 |
| Self-doubt | Beat self-doubt with self-affirmation. Defeat every | Psalms 139:13-14 |

| | | |
|---|---|---|
| | negative thought with God's word. For example, when you feel doubt about your look, tell yourself that you are God's masterpiece. | |
| Fear | Fear is faith in the wrong direction. Use the same energy to believe the good outcome is eminent instead of the bad, and watch what happens! | Joshua 1:9 |
| Ungodly Entertainment | Walk with airphones! As far as possible always have the option of blocking out content that is not for you, if you can't leave a space. | Titus 2:12 |
| Failures | You truly haven't experienced great success if you haven't gone through a failure. Failures will come but God promised that everything | Romans 8:28 |

| | | |
|---|---|---|
| | will work out for our good. Brush those failures off, start over or just keep it moving. | |
| Issues with Family | You are your own individual. You can control your actions and reactions. You can't control others. With this perspective, we take responsibility for what we can control and leave other persons to account for themselves | 1 Corinthians 13:4-8 |
| Drug abuse | Never underestimate the power of leaning on someone else's shoulder. More people want to help you than you realize. | 1 Peter 1:13 |
| Pride | Pride is absolutely useless. Swallow the pride and ask for help. Swallow | James 4:6 |

| | the pride and assist someone who is in need. Swallow the pride and worship God the way you want to. | |
|---|---|---|
| Not knowing how to pray | Talk to Him like you would your best friend. Sometimes you'll have a lot to say and sometimes you won't. Let him know what's bothering you, let him know what you need clarity on. He takes the rest from there, trust me. | Romans 8: 26 |

God told the Israelites in Jeremiah 29:11 that He knows the plans He has for them, plans to prosper them and not to harm them, plans to give them hope and a future. I believe He is saying the same thing to us today.

God knew we would face these trials. He knew we would feel like we are not strong enough, and that is why He gave us these words to comfort us. He wants us to understand that the pressures we are facing now are actually the tools which, if used properly, will lead us to that ultimate goal which is to receive the crown of life.

Have you ever imagined that day, that day when God says, "Well done good and faithful servant?" Amazing, isn't it? It is like going through High School or University for four or five years with sleepless nights, hardly any fun, missing out on special activities and constantly needing to relax. At the end of it all, it's an amazing feeling when that journey has ended and you walk across that stage to collect your certificate. It's pretty much the same thing with our Christian lives. We have to go through many trials before ultimately receiving the great reward.

There will always be a light at the end of the tunnel in every situation you face because God says He has plans to prosper you. Think about Job. He lost almost everything, in one day! Fortunately, he knew the God he served, kept the faith and God rewarded him in the end. God gave him more than he had in previous times. Take comfort in knowing that you are never alone and that God always rescues His children. The three Hebrew boys faced a difficult situation too. They were thrown in the fiery furnace - they experienced neither damage nor pain because God rescued them. You may feel like you are in a fiery furnace today and have started to think that you are going under, that you are going to fail, or that you are going to die. But I have good news for you! You are surrounded by angels and you have been rescued by your heavenly Father.

Sometimes as young Christians we yield to the pressures we face and then we are so taken over by guilt that we think God has turned His back on us. In the story of the Prodigal Son in Luke 15, the son was very disloyal to his father and he thought that his father would never forgive him. His father did forgive him. In fact, his daddy was waiting with open arms. Just like the father in this story, God is waiting with His arms wide open. He wants you to know that He will never turn his back on you. He just wants you to repent and seek his forgiveness.

Do not be discouraged by the pressures you face. Instead, be grateful! Yes, be grateful because you will be amazed at how those same pressures help you to develop valuable skills which will aid you in your breakthrough and contribute to your overall growth and maturity.

I encountered particular social issues that I know produced specific Christian values. In the moment it was hard, but on the other side, I was better than before. Here are some lessons I learnt that may be true for you too.

| Issue | Lesson |
| --- | --- |
| Failures | Teaches patience and forces us to think harder and grow. It invites us to do better next time. |
| Death and sickness | This one is a tough teacher, but it teaches us the value of life. These kinds of experiences remind us |

|  |  |
|---|---|
|  | that time belongs to no one and encourages us not to take life for granted. |
| Criticism or Bullying | Teaches us to distinguish our identity from what people say to what God says. It promotes a strong backbone and a resolve to remain peaceful even when provoked. |
| Experiencing lack | Not having enough in a season, teaches us to be grateful. The true believer will depend on their God to provide all their needs no matter how abundant or sparce their resources are. |
| Sadness | Being sad is difficult. But it teaches us that true joy is from above and that we can choose to be happy. |

I started writing this book before I was faced with the challenge of my exam failure. I prayed continually for wisdom, understanding and knowledge, but how could I get these without going through some trials? Sometimes our trials become so overwhelming that we forget what we asked God for. God had to take me through some hard times. He had to let some people leave.

God demanded my attention harder than He ever did to equip me for the next dimension of my journey. God was preparing me. He was making me a better version of me! Has it ever dawned on you that your trials will be your testimony someday and that God will finish the good work He started in you? We should find comfort in knowing that though these trials may be painful in the moment, they work for our good. When making your plans, make way for God's will. When facing your trials, know that He means you no ill, and when it seems like all hope is gone, stand firm knowing you will overcome, be better, and ultimately please God's heart.

# CHAPTER 2

# HOW TO OVERCOME

"When you go through deep waters, I will be with you." Isaiah 43:2 (NLT)

I went to a youth retreat a few months after receiving my results and the theme was "Get into Gear, It's Shifting Season". One of the speakers said "You can move from one location to another or move from out of a situation physically but if your mindset isn't shifted then you haven't really moved". That statement hit me like a ton of bricks. It dawned on me that merely brushing my previous failures aside did not mean that I recovered or more importantly, that I learnt from them. Though I had moved physically, mentally I was still enslaved by those moments. I say this to say, recovery and overcoming, all starts with the mind.

The Pressures of this life sometimes seem impossible and unfair. We face death, loss, ostracization, financial hardship, sickness, and so much more. We feel at times that we are unable to overcome. Remember in the previous chapter I spoke about experiencing a major failure in my life and being depressed for months? During that time, I smiled, but it was fake. I laughed a lot but honestly, I was crying hard on the inside for help.

It was hard to overcome what I was going through because my mind was filled with so many negative thoughts. I thought that I was a failure. I doubted that I could ever be successful in life. I began to listen to my own negative self-talk and began to live from that place of internal blame. With the disappointment that I still felt, I was at a low, low place.

But in a moment of calm and clarity, I considered my depressed state and wondered whether there may be other things that made me feel so down and distressed. Over time, with the help of the Holy Spirit, I realized that this overwhelming feeling was also caused by the failures that had traumatized me in the past. With this painful, honest confession, healing and overcoming had begun.

## COLLIECIA'S 3 STEPS TO OVERCOMING
## SPEAK TO YOUR MIND

*If your negative mindset isn't changed, you will never overcome.* As Christians, our minds should be in covenant with the word of God, remembering that the word of God exposes the promises of God. So even though the pressures we face seem unbearable sometimes, we should fill our minds with the word of God instead of filling it with negative thoughts. In doing this we will be reminded of the promises of God. So, when we hear the thought that "I am a disappointment" lingering in our minds, we will replace it with the thought of "I am loved" because God says He loves us. When we hear "I am a failure" it will be replaced with "I am chosen" because God says so. When the thought "This problem is drowning me" enslaves our mind, it will be eradicated by the promise that all things will work together for my good. We have to change our mindsets so that they are in alignment with God's words. Remember always that his promises are "Yes" and "Amen".

## PRAY – HONESTLY AND OFTEN

The second step to overcoming the pressures we face is to pray. Prayer is one of the first things that the devil tries to steal when we fall into the pressure of guilt after sinning. We feel overwhelmed and are convinced that God is distant and so we enter into a kind of futile malice with God! We isolate the one power that can heal and forgive us. This is a trap of the enemy. It is in these moments that we must run to God quickly and sincerely to confess and to invite him to help us to change our ways. The longer we delay this vital process, the longer we are bound by our situation.

God is listening out for our prayers. To be frank, talking to God just makes everything a whole lot better. One would think that the first step should be to pray but you can't pray until your mindset is changed. Remember, we can't fool God. So, if you pray with a negative mindset, then your prayer will never be effective.

Even if we don't have all the answers and we still have some doubt, we must have faith! Faith comes from a change of mind. God knows what we are going through but it is our belief, even if its reluctant, it is our belief that God can help us that produces sincere prayer. Cry out to God! Show Him how desperately you want to be rescued and don't ever think that He's not there. He is right there knocking on your heart's door. Will you let him in?

I remembered when I stopped praying because I was so upset with God. The Lord reminded me that He was right there whenever I was ready and so I gradually changed my mindset. I started praying again because I was desperately in need of rescue. I cried unto the Lord and He reminded me again and again, that He was right there. Truth is, He never left!

I've learnt, that when there is a conflict in a relationship and you want it to be resolved you have to listen to each other. It is the same way when we are communicating with God. When we cry out and pray to him, we should also listen to what He has to say. I became closer to God when I started listening to Him. Listening to God is a major part of the solution to all the challenges we face.

So, ensure that your mindset is changed and while you pray, listen.

## TRIM YOUR CIRCLE

When God moves someone out of our lives, we should be less quick to believe that he has taken something from us. Often, God has given us access to growth, blessings and abundance that that person's influence may have been blocking. God knows what is best for us! Having the right people on your team makes overcoming pressures a lot easier. In my dark moments, some people left but those who stayed proved to be just who I needed on my team. They cried with me, they fought my sadness and distress with me and they reminded me every single day that I was going to be okay.

There is no purer form of love than someone who prays for you. That is what my true friends did. In life we will meet a lot of people and we may ask the question "How do I know if this person means me well?" Ask God. Believe me, God will reveal everything to you in due time. Your people will always help you to carry your cross whether they are near or far away. They will not judge your sorrow or your errors, but will have compassion and pray with you.

Ask God for the spirit of discernment, so you can discover all the things you need to see in the spiritual realm. Even as youth, God will send us signs in our language, cultural and age appropriate platforms that tell us exactly what we need to know about the people around us. Sarah Jakes Roberts said "When you can't walk away from the relationship, God will make the relationship walk away from you". God is a creative and multi-faceted Father. He will organize your life according to his divine purpose if you let him. You can overcome whatever you are facing.

Change your mindset, Pray and listen to God and ensure you have the right people on your team. Remember always that God will be with you through the deepest of waters that you face and therefore they will not overwhelm you.

# CHAPTER 3

# THE BALANCE

"Therefore, my beloved brothers, be steadfast, immovable, always abounding in the work of the Lord, knowing that your labor in the Lord is not in vain." 1 Corinthians 15:58 (ESV)

Regardless of the outcome, never forget that what you do for Christ will last. Often we ask God, "Why did you give me this gift?" At times we become so overwhelmed by the pressure of balancing the work that comes with the gift. Another question we may ask is "Why does my life have to be so hard?" I find that sometimes this is because we have to make difficult decisions.

A simple but prime example is deciding whether to stay home and study for final exams or go to church to fulfill commitments to serve. Seems simple? Perhaps. But it's the same thought process that an older person may make between working late for their family, or making it in time for evening services. This can be a very uncomfortable place to be in but ultimately, it all comes back to what we prioritize the most. Do we want to prioritize the degree or do we want to prioritize eternal life? How can we create space so that we still provide for our family, while fulfilling our obligations at church? These are tough questions, but the strategies we create in our youth often create patterns that we follow in our later years. It's always useful to remember that Jesus sacrificed his life for our sins. He didn't have to do it but He did because He loves us. That thought usually sets everything in startling perspective.

Balance is not only a decision to be in one place versus another, it is a commitment. Our dedication to God's work is a part of our sacrifice and while it may be overwhelming sometimes, we should continue toiling. Always remember that even though the cross was heavy, Jesus carried it all the way, for your sake and mine. The job, the degree, the parties, they will all fade away but what we do for God, that will last. Furthermore, when we put God's work above all else, he gives generously to us from his abundance.

I can tell you from my experience that your gift can become overwhelming at times. As younger members of a body, we often find it difficult to say no even when we feel overwhelmed and exhausted. It is important to gauge your mental health and your true capacity without feeling guilty or ashamed. Even though you may be young, your schedule and planning is important too! On the other hand, there were many times that I had presentations at school on a Monday morning and was also asked to participate in ministry activity at church the Sunday morning before that. Truth be told, I was tempted many times to stay home and work on my presentation but I didn't give in. I still went to church, did what I had to do and I did extremely well on my presentation the next morning. I say this to say, that God will never let you fail. Be honest with others and with yourself, do all that you can for Christ, and He will take care of the rest.

As for entertainment and other social activities in this balancing act, there is so much to look forward to when we throw ourselves into things of God. While parties are touted as fun and touted as the best time of your life, there's an even greater party in the kingdom. I've been around unsaved friends who love to party and live what they call 'their best lives' but I never ever thought that I was missing out because I was so filled up with all the activities available in the church. Furthermore, volunteer groups and other community activities are other exciting considerations for socializing and entertainment.

The joy of a party only lasts for a few hours but what you gain when you are in the presence of God will last forever. When we can help others, care for the sick, host concerts and parties where no one feels awful afterwards, we grow and evolve socially and emotionally. We develop healthy traits that complement our Christian walk rather than offend it.

As for me personally, my mantra for balance is a bit simple but not simplistic. It is this: Choose God and everything else will fall into place. Now while more care will be given as I get older concerning exactly what this looks like in practical operation, what I can say definitively, is that using this phrase as the basis of my decision-making and balancing act hasn't failed me yet!

Whenever you find yourself fighting to find balance between your Christian life and other important areas of your life, just know that imbalance is not of God. God desires that as we please him and grow spiritually, that other elements of our life will grow and prosper as well. Do not give in to anxiety and imbalance. Choose to focus on Christ before all things, and success and favour will be yours, even in the midst of challenges.

# CHAPTER 4

# WALKING BOLDLY AS YOUNG CHRISTIANS

"For the Spirit God gave us does not make us timid, but gives us power, love and self-discipline." 2 Timothy 1:7 (NIV)

I remember the first time I did a sermon at church. I was so nervous! I almost backed out of the task but I prayed about it and I became bold even though I didn't know what I was going into! God showed up and showed off in the service. All I can say is that I'm still blown away by how God used me that day.

What if I had followed that timid feeling? I would not have been used by God and that person who needed the word, would not have received it. Sometimes we may not be sure what we're getting ourselves into but still take that bold step. You never know what God wants to do with you many times. Unless you try, you may not know what is your unique gift.

~~~

Along our Christian journey, after some inspirational event or some other significant breakthrough, many of us may make a commitment like, "God, I'm going to be bolder than I have ever been!" Well, that is very easy to say. However, as we continue on our journey with Christ, we realize it's much harder to do.

Many young Christians, and even older followers, allow timidity to either cause us to forget or renege on that bold commitment. We become timid because we realize that it's harder than we thought. In 2 Timothy 1:7, God says that He has not given us a spirit of fear. This means that timidity could only come from the enemy.

God made each of us with our own unique gifts and because our God is so great, we know these gifts aren't ordinary. The enemy sees this and he also sees that this will contribute to the destruction of his kingdom of darkness. For this reason, among others, we cannot be timid in our walk with Christ! We have to be bold. If we refuse to be bold in our Christian walk, it's almost as though we are handing our power and authority to the enemy on a silver platter. We cannot allow the kingdom of darkness to overcome us.

Sometimes as young Christians we start functioning in an area in which we believe we are gifted but give up fairly quickly because we have a rough start. That should never be the case. Rough starts do not indicate a lack of God's leadership. Often, we must grow into our gift and learn difficult lessons to become better stewards of our gift.

God would never put us in a situation or present a gift to us that He hasn't already prepared us for. Sometimes we have to grow into our gifts and a part of growing in our gifts is being bold. So even though you may have fallen when doing your first dance or your voice cracked during your first solo, don't be fearful of doing the second performance. Instead, be bold and minister like you never messed up in the first round.

Being bold will attract challenges. People will criticize you. Your gift may put you in a ministry led by a not-so-nice leader or you may experience injuries in areas needed for you to minister with your gifts. Yes, these will all come but I promise you, just stay in the course and you'll see how much your confidence will grow. It will grow so much that it will cause you to excel in spite of all the challenges faced. When using our God-given and unique gifts we cannot be timid. We have to be bold, so that the message we deliver is most effective.

Within new giftings and new purpose, we often must learn step by step. If we fall, we should simply try again. It is similar to being in a race. If you fall, get up, brush yourself off and keep running. God isn't concerned with how we place in the races set before us. He is considered with how well each of us finish. My finish will be different from yours because we had different experiences along the way. But finish we must, and finish well -with our faith and Christian integrity intact, to the glory of God.

Some may ask the question, "How do I become bold?" There's one answer to that. You should trust God enough to take you through whatever you are fearful of facing or doing. As soon as you make the decision to start walking with Christ, the devil starts planning his schemes to get you to stop or to distract you. You have to be prepared for this. If you are not bold, Satan will overpower you easily. Might I remind you that God said He has given us power. You have the power within you but in order for this power to be effective, you have to bring life to it with your boldness.

Sometimes you are in a big crowd and you sense a difference in the atmosphere and you feel the urge to shout hallelujah, shout it! It may feel awkward but you don't know what that hallelujah is chasing away. You may be in your classroom and you feel the need to pray, do it! It could be very uncomfortable but put your pride aside and pray. Your prayer could be cancelling a plan the enemy has in motion.

We ask God to use us but we cannot be used by God until we unleash our boldness. One day I went to school and I saw my principal and I kept on hearing a voice saying "Go pray for her". I ignored the voice for days. I thought, "My principal! No I can't do that!" A week or so later, I heard that she was ill. I was so upset with myself. I allowed my pride to get in the way of my boldness. I couldn't help but think that her circumstances may have been different if I'd gone and prayed for her. Maybe she would not have ended up in the hospital or fallen ill. Maybe if I prayed with her like God had asked me to, whatever the enemy had in store would have been cancelled. From that day I vowed that I would never think twice about what God asks me to do, even if it's going to make me uncomfortable.

To be completely bold in our walk with Christ, we are going to have to get uncomfortable sometimes. My friend, be bold! It won't be easy but put your pride away. Put away second-guessing yourself and trust God to take you through. We all want to be used by God. No one wants to be stagnant. But in order for that to happen, we have to be bold. Unleash that boldness and let God use you the way He wants to.

# CHAPTER 5

# MAKING AN IMPACT

"Let your light so shine before men, that they may see your good works and glorify your father which is in heaven." Matthew 5:16 (KJV)

The way we live our Christian lives should always make an impact. If we are not making an impact by the way we live then we should do some soul-searching to see where we have lost our salt according to Matthew 5:13. Quite frankly, we are no ordinary people; we are children of God and the light that God is shining through us should always impact someone or something.

Perhaps we are not allowing that light to shine because we are covering it up with the blanket of doubt, unforgiveness, ungodly entertainment, lack of study, sometimes even fleshly desires like fornication and lust among other things. We can't be living a godly and ungodly lifestyle at the same time. You can't have one foot in and one foot out. That will surely dim the light that God is trying to shine through us.

Often, God places people in our lives so we can shine our light on them. Many times we don't realize that this is the case and we fail to realize that the person is looking to us as an example. If we choose to live the one foot in, one foot out lifestyle then that person will never experience the light of our great God. They will tend to adopt the same lifestyle we're living because they will think that it's okay to live that way.

We impact people directly and indirectly. This is why it is important to live a Christian life that makes a positive impact. We cannot afford to be a stumbling-block to those outside of the faith or a bad example to those within the faith. We must be circumspect before God, but also before our fellow man.

To make a positive impact, we cannot be like everyone else. We cannot join others listening to ungodly music or watching ungodly videos even if it means we are odd. Not everyone believes in God, but He declared that every knee will bow and every tongue will confess that He is God. What if He's raising us up to make this fact be known among our peers, within our country or across the world? If we do not live a life of example, we may miss what God is doing because we choose not to separate ourselves from an ungodly lifestyle. Separate yourself!

You can't be like everyone else; you can't stay here and do your own thing, because you came on business for the King. Some of us could have been dead but we're alive today because we need to be making an impact with the Christian life that we are living. We need to let our light shine so brightly that others may see His good works and glorify

God in heaven. What if Saul ignored the signs God gave him to change the way he was living in Acts 9? He would not have won souls for God.

Living a lukewarm life reflects unbelief. It demonstrates a lack of trust in God. When our lifestyles are inconsistent, we insult God. We set a bad example of God's standards and may cause others looking on to form erroneous conclusions about God and his people at large.

Specifically, when we are unkind, or full of anger and unforgiveness, or we enter sinful relationships or go to clubs, gamble and give in to drunkenness we misrepresent God. We cause shame to His name because our actions are not in line with His standards of holiness. When there is no distinction between us and our friends who are not Christians, we give the impression that God's commandments aren't really important. While they may come to know Jesus as Saviour, they may think that it is okay to live an ungodly lifestyle because we portrayed it as something that could be tolerated by God.

When we do this, not only do we distort the light that God is shining through us, but we also allow ourselves to become barriers to that light being shined in and through others. Let this be a reminder today of how valuable we are to God's kingdom. If you have one foot out, today I encourage you to put it right back in. You have work to do. Get to work and ensure you make an impact while doing it. God's counting on YOU!

# CHAPTER 6

# MAINTAINING A FUELED CHRISTIAN LIFE

"Those who are planted in the house of the Lord shall flourish in the courts of our God." Psalm 92:13 (NKJV)

Youthful exuberance in the work of Christ must be tempered with loving coaching and compassionate mentorship. Because our issues are valid, and our energy levels are so high, as youth, we run the risk of running out of gas. Additionally, when youth apply themselves wholeheartedly to the work of God and to positive activities like education, volunteering and wholesome entertainment, we become target of the enemy. It is important then, as young Christians, to persist in refilling our spiritual tanks and in seeking our faith authentically and personally.

I learnt this critical lesson in perhaps one of the most transitional and transformative years of my life and in the life of many other young adults and people overall! You see, it was time to take on a new journey. I thought I had experienced enough and that now I would be getting a break from the trials and pressures of my earlier years. But my, O my, was I wrong!

## The Evolution of Young Christians

It was August 2020, a year after the traumatic August of 2019. I thought, certainly in 2020, I would be able to cruise into the exciting season of university. I had dreamt of this moment and now, after failure, perseverance and eventual victory in my studies, it was time for the great adventure of tertiary education.

I applied for many scholarships and grants but was denied every last one as the pandemic crippled funds and forced many donors to renege on their offers as everyone responded to the uncertainty of the time. Those random miracles where God would send someone with some cash to bless me, never materialized. It was happening all over again, another setback. I fell into a place that I wanted to forget but with which I was now far too familiar. I was in despair. I cried to God and hoped deep down that come the next morning he would work something out – amazingly. But it didn't happen. I was locked away at home with my prospect of university slipping into a strange distant place that was even further compounded by a global pandemic. "Just my luck!" I thought despondently.

The oddity and despair of this period took me back to Christmas morning some years back when mother and I went to church hoping that God would give us a Christmas miracle. We had no money, we had no food, we had no gas, all we had was each other. That morning after giving thanks for a Christ we already had, we went home without food, which was what we really needed at the time, in that moment. As our empty stomachs growled in protest, we said grace over some leftover ackee from the night before and commanded our souls not to worry.

It is a dark place such as that place to which I felt I was returning. I will tell you, that I almost fell into that cycle. I almost gave into the feeling and the memories. But with those bad memories came the memory of how God came through for me. The memory of how I didn't die from hunger, how help didn't come in the morning when we expected it but surely by evening, He was there. I called to the front of my mind, how when I had failed before, God had spoken to me and delivered my mind from believing I was a failure.

I realized that having triumphed over that period, I had become a bit inconsistent with my devotion to God. You see, sometimes when we have moved past our struggles, we feel the clarity of the moment but neglect the dedication needed for the moment to come. We go on living as though we lose some of our desperation for God when his blessings flow. We become complacent and forgetful. Sometimes, God gets our attention, not from daily communing as He should, but through a difficulty that drives us to pray and read His word.

Our life is like a moving vehicle, the gas that is in it cannot last forever no matter how full we feel after a particular season. As we move on in our daily lives, we need a different word, a different blessing, because what we had was for that time, that season. We must continue praying or we will start to forget the power of the God we serve! We must continue reading the Word of God else we will start forgetting the promises of God! That my friends, is how we stay fueled. We must never forget to remain in communion with God.

As for my immediate issue of school, is He not Jehovah Jireh? Am I not his child? Of course, he provided for me! He proved once again how awesome He was and is. I was ready and energized to take on the world again because God came through on the buzzer and helped me to access my first semester. I thought, "Well surely now I can relax and begin school. No more worries." How naïve of me, for the difficulties had only just began. I mean, I knew it was going to be challenging. I expected it to test my intellect. But! This exceeded my expectations. With the pandemic at play, school became this new, weird puzzle to pick up and figure out. I cried almost every day of the week from frustration. It seemed like the entire world was on my shoulders and when I did not get my A+ for some of my assignments, I was quite distressed.

Here we were again! I was feeling frustrated and discouraged. Then, as before, I paused and thought, "When was the last time I did not rush a prayer and really stayed on my knees and talked to my God? I had gotten so busy with meeting deadlines, I had gotten so busy working for that A+, I had gotten so busy with pleasing these lecturers with great quality work, that I forgot to focus on who and what really mattered.

Now, I am not saying that education is not important. But what really is success without God? You see, I recognized why I was so flustered and annoyed. I was lacking gas. I was still depending on the gas I was filled up with months ago. The tank was empty, I had nothing left. I was slacking in my devotion. This was the problem. But the power was lying in my hands to fix it. I had to get back on track. I had to start setting my reminders again to read my Bible, to pause the essay-typing and start praying again. You see, I had to start working on my A+ for communicating with my Maker. Changes had to be made so differences could be felt.

## Here are some other useful ways to Maintain a Fueled Christian Life

### GO TO THAT RETREAT

Remember in Chapter 2 where I mentioned going to a youth retreat? That retreat did a lot for me. I released what I needed to let go of and I made room for what I needed to grow. Being part of these activities, if you allow it, exposes what is laying deep on the inside.

I remembered when I first heard about retreats, I was immediately turned off. I thought, "What would this weekend do for me anyways?" But it did so much! My first retreat was nothing short of amazing, I remembered going there confused and questioning what the outcome of the weekend would be. It felt so odd. This was a new environment, and even though I knew most of the persons I was surrounded by, there were a few that I had to get used to. I got over that phase and then it was time to attend the sessions. I wanted to sleep and I thought the sessions would put me back to bed but surprisingly they didn't. I was hooked! It was like God told these speakers all about my life! They said everything I needed to hear. I could remember one speaker distinctly saying to me, "You're confused, but I pray that the Lord gives you understanding." I was shocked! I could not believe what I heard.

The Lord desired for me to have a fueled Christian life and he would do whatever it took for me to have this same desire. I remember after that experience, I completely surrendered and my life has never been the same since. Whenever I go back to retreats, it's never a problem for me to fully open my heart and receive whatever God has in store. Every year I have attended, I never left the same. I always left with the fuel I needed to carry me on through my journey. The different power-packed sessions with the various amazing speakers, the girl talks, the fun activities, all allowed me to feel free and to let go of what was keeping me bound so I could make way for the fuel I needed to go on.

## JOIN AN ONLINE GROUP

Maybe you're not like me who wants to spend a whole weekend away from home. Perhaps you just want to stay in the comfort of your home and receive the fuel that you so desperately need. If that's you, join an online group. Create a prayer chat or a bible study. There are always opportunities to connect to others and to God. Even though I have my own church, I decided that it might not be a bad thing to be part of an online church as well. I found a group online where I connected with others to discuss specific subjects and to share how it impacts our personal lives. Sometimes the discussion gets so interesting that we even forget that we are following a specific guide. I always leave full, refreshed and ready to conquer whatever lies ahead. It changed my life for the better and not only will I have friends for a lifetime, but I'll always have nuggets to reflect on whenever I get weary.

## GET INVOLVED!

Get involved in church activities. If you can sing, join the choir. If you can speak well, join the communications team. If you can dance well, join the dance ministry, and the list goes on. From the age of 8 years old I've always been involved and I have realized that when I become weary, being engaged in ministry has given me courage to push past my struggles.

## HAVE AN ACCOUNTABILITY PARTNER

Having an accountability partner is everything. Someone who ensures that you are doing what you promised you would do. It is understandable that sometimes life does get hectic and you forget some of the things you set out to do. But when your accountability partner is really in your corner, they will remind you that you've got some unfinished business to take care of. Those persons you post every day and caption them to be your best friend or your ride or die, let them hold you accountable. Share your goals with them, share your struggles with them and let them help you on this journey of maintaining a fueled Christian life.

Bear in mind though, that sometimes the person you call your best friend can turn out to be your very worst enemy – leading you astray rather than closer to God. So, consult God first before assigning this role. To make things easier, you can also be that friend's accountability partner too. This way, not only are you being held accountable, you are holding someone accountable as well. I know it may not be easy for you to be absolutely transparent or vulnerable concerning issues, struggles and hardships, but if you really want a fueled life, you will do what it takes.

I didn't really pay attention to the things I promised to myself until I got an accountability partner. Pretty quickly, I realized I did not want to be scolded by my partner when I told them I did not do as I promised. I wanted to feel like I was making some progress and I wanted my accountability partner to express pride and support towards my efforts rather than expressing disappointment. I say all this to say, speaking from experience, having an accountability partner isn't so bad at all. In fact, it can be life-changing. Try it.

## SEEK OUT A MENTOR

Finally, get a mentor. My mother always tells me, sometimes you think you know everything, but you really don't. So, I am telling you now, sometimes we think we know it all, but we really don't. Get a mentor, or speak to your youth group to assign one to you. Some relationships will work out, and some won't. But try just the same. The potential value of this arrangement far outweighs the risk.

It won't hurt to talk things out with someone, especially someone you trust. Be very open and honest because if you aren't, then it will seem like nothing is working out. Your mentor can't read minds, they can't know what's going on. The ball is in your court to speak up. Sometimes our mentors have gone through what we are going through and they can tell us what to do and what not to do. Turn off the lightbulb of pride and allow someone who actually has knowledge of the challenges you encounter to guide you. I can clearly remember the moments I felt like I was falling off track, but speaking to someone changed the outcome that was about to transpire. If it worked for me, it can for you too. However, you have to be willing to allow that to happen by being honest and receptive. Get a mentor! There's nothing to be afraid of. Do you want to be better or do you want your tank to remain empty?

~~~

Maintaining a fueled Christian life is very important, for what is a car without gas? No matter how fancy, or how new the model, it is only a showpiece, not fulfilling any of its true purpose, if it has no gas to move. I have shared experiences with you, but I've also shared solutions. I pray that you will do some serious evaluation on your own life and decide whether or not you want to keep your car moving. You see, God has made the fuel available for us, and there are no restrictions on it. It is only for us to make use of it.

# CONCLUDING STATEMENTS

"Farther along we'll know all about it,
Farther along we'll understand why.
Cheer up my brothers [and sisters],
Live in the sunshine;
We'll understand it all by and by."

The journey of Evolving as a young Christian is not easy, but I promise you that it will be worth it. You will have a few bumps on the journey but with God by your side you will be successful. Remember always, that in life you will never stop evolving, even when you have evolved as a young Christian, the evolution of your life continues.

I pray that this book has blessed you richly and that you will do some evaluation on your life, so we can evolve together and cause a Christ-led revolution among our families and our communities.

May God bless you always.

# NOTES

www.ingramcontent.com/pod-product-compliance
Lightning Source LLC
Chambersburg PA
CBHW061255040426
42444CB00010B/2384